SCALES OF THE BLACK SERPENT

Basic Qlippothic Magick
The Order of Phosphorus

MICHAEL W. FORD
WITH DUALKARNAIN

TITLES BY MICHAEL W. FORD
www.luciferianwitchcraft.com

THE BIBLE OF THE ADVERSARY
LUCIFERIAN WITCHCRAFT
SATANIC MAGICK: A Paradigm of Therion
GATES OF DOZAK: Primal Sorcery
THE VAMPIRE GATE: The Vampyre Magickian
BOOK OF THE WITCH MOON
THE FIRST BOOK OF LUCIFERIAN TAROT
LUCIFERIAN TAROT
LUCIFERIAN GOETIA: A Book of Howling
ADAMU: Luciferian Sex Magick
LIBER HVHI: Magick of the Adversary
AKHKHARU – VAMPYRE MAGICK
MAGICK OF THE ANCIENT GODS

SCALES OF THE BLACK SERPENT

Basic Qlippothic Magick

The foundations and essential ideological foundation of Working with the Qlippoth as founded by THE ORDER OF PHOSPHORUS and associative Grade Workings.

BY

MICHAEL W. FORD
AKHTYA DAHAK V°
With Dualkarnain

SCALES OF THE BLACK SERPENT
Basic Qlippothic Magick
By Michael W. Ford

Copyright © 2009 by Michael W. Ford

All rights reserved. No part of this book, in part or in whole, may be reproduced, transmitted, or utilized, in any form or by any means electronic or mechanical, including photocopying, recording, or by any information storage and retrieval system, without written permission in writing from the publisher, except for brief quotations in critical articles, books and reviews.

First edition 2009 Succubus Productions
ISBN 978-0-578-03410-2

Information:

Succubus Productions
PO Box 926344
Houston, TX 77292
USA

Website: http://www.luciferianwitchcraft.com
email: succubusproductions@yahoo.com

TABLE OF CONTENTS

Forward...................Page 11

PART ONE: Theory and Preparation

The Qlippoth & Tree of Da'ath................Page 15

Structure of TOPH Grades & Qlippothic Correspondence......Page 16

Realm of the Qlippoth..................Page 17

Demonic Rulers and Names of Power.................Page 19

Nature of Magickal Energy.............Page 20

Foundation..............Page 21

Magickial Instruments of Darksome Art...............Page 21

The Circle of the Adversary......................Page 22

The Triangle of Evocation......................Page 23

Incense........................Page 24

PART TWO: Invocations

Luciferian Trinity Invocation (Banishing & Focusing)..........Page 27

The Fallen Angelick Conjuration..................Page 29

Qlippothic Prayers...............Page 31

PART THREE: The Qlippoth and the Tree of Da'ath

Malkuth & Nahemoth......................Page 39

Yesod & Lilith......................Page 41

Hod & Samael.................Page 43

Netzach & Harab-Serapel...................Page 45

Tipheth & Tagaririm......................Page 49

Geburah & Golab............................Page 51

Chesed & Gamichicoth.........................Page 53

Daath and Choronzon......................Page 55

Binah & Satariel............................Page 57

Chokmah & Chaigidel....................Page 59

Kether & Thaumiel......................Page 61

7

THE CROWN OF GODS, The Devil Qemetiel Above Kether....Page 63

PART FOUR: The Zodiack and the Qlippoth.........Page 65

PART FIVE: The Order of Phosphorus……………...Page 83

BIBLOGRAPHY

PART ONE:
THEORY AND PREPARATION

FORWARD

The grimoire will provide some foundation for not only The Qlippoth, yet also The Order of Phosphorus and the aim of the order. TOPH has been an expanding guild for several years and operates with the Guidance of The Black Order of the Dragon, a Vampyric Temple which has existed since 1993. TOPH itself has been on a continual development phase since its inception in early 2002, expanding upon the Luciferian ideology and Magickial (the added "I" in Magick-i-al has a specific reference to A.O. Spare) workings, the Luciferian path has and is changing and transforming lives via the Left Hand Path.

This grimoire is a basic; stripped down expansion of some foundational Qlippothic texts contained in "The Bible of the Adversar", "Liber HVHI" and others which fueled TOPH.

This grimoire should be used to challenge and inspire your own inner and outer transformation within the Luciferian Path. The Order of Phosphorus offers a gateway, yet it is up to the Black Adept to go forward through the gateway.

The Order of Phosphorus understands that someone who has a strong Will may create a meaningful and productive life, the Black Adept of TOPH understands that the Luciferian is a perfect example of this; self-accountability, honesty, strength of mind and having achievable goals are all examples of purpose and the enduring focus of the initiate.

We view the universe are being composed of "waves" of energy, that humanity itself creates and adds to the direction of the energy in certain aspects. The Black Adept can tap into these hidden worlds, the Qlippoth and singularly "empower" the subconscious and fill the "shells" of the dark regions.

The Three types of Luciferian Magick – Therionick Sorcery – Bestial, lycanthropic, lustful and chaotic self-exploration workings, Yatukih Sorcery – primal, compelling acts of expanding influence in the world, based on the foundation of the Yatuk Dinoih and other ancient inverse Zoroastrian texts in "The Bible of the Adversary", "Luciferian Witchcraft" and "Gates of Dozak" among others and Luciferian Magick – transformative inner high sorcery, or theurgy. Luciferian Magick is the union of the Daemon or ones Holy Guardian Angel.

The Qlippoth, a centered foundation to The Order of Phosphorus will liberate any Magickian to a new paradigm of thought – no longer needing or approaching any Judeo-Christian God, the Luciferian adopts the perception of the Fallen Angels and Archetypes of individuality and self-liberation to ascend just as they, knowing both darkness and light in a balanced perspective.

I would like to thank Dualkarnain for graciously offering his Qlippothic Prayers from Malkuth to Netzach.

In addition I would like to thank Mr. Sasse for his detailed suggestion concerning the Qlippoth.

Thank you to Priestess Satrina especially for her support.

Honor to all initiates of TOPH, you will reshape the world in our darkness and blackened light!

Those interested in The Order of Phosphorus may seek us at www.theorderofphosphorus.com or www.luciferianwitchcraft.com at the time of writing.

Ba nãm i âharman
Michael W. Ford - Akhtya Dahak V°
The Order of Phosphorus

Lucifer-Satan by Dore

ARCH-DEMONS & Qlippothic Orders

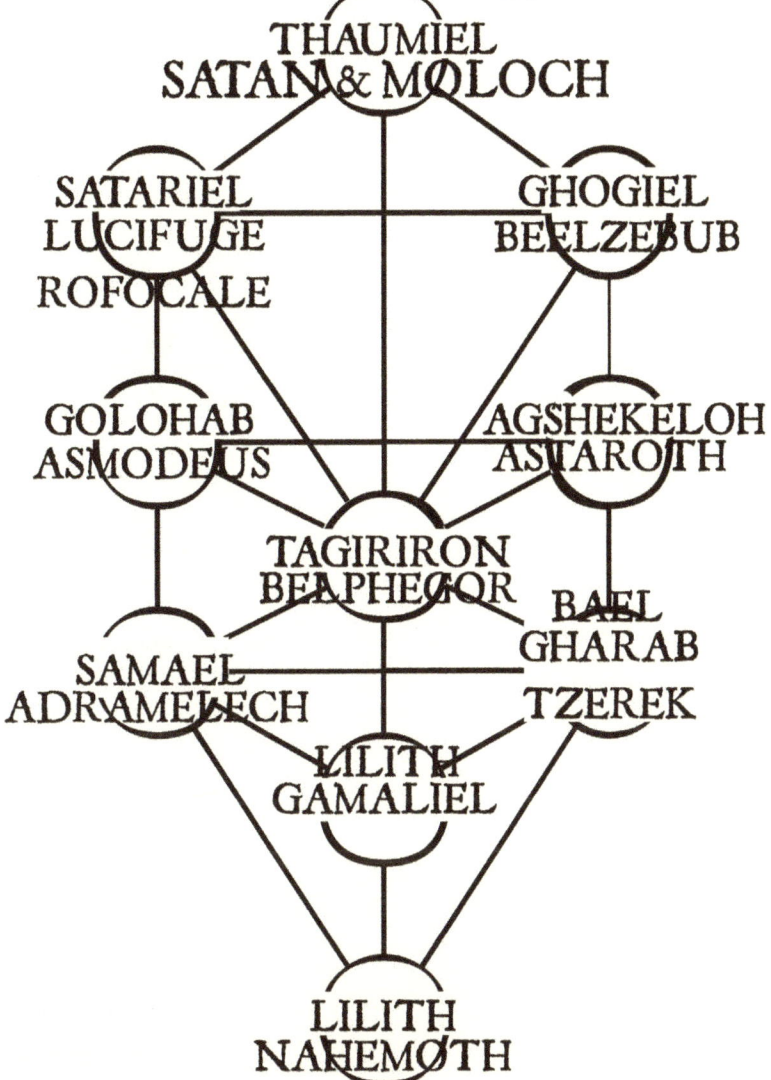

The Qlippoth & Tree of Da'ath

THE ORDER OF PHOSPHORUS

Number	Order of Demons	Planet and Sphere	TOPH	Initiatory
10	Thamiel	Kether	Grade V - Magus	Manifestation of the Adversary
9	Chaigidel	Chokmah	Grade V - Magus	Manifestation of the Adversary
8	Sathariel	Binah - Saturn	Grade III – IV	Will of the Adversary
7	Gamchicoth	Chesed - Jupiter	Grade II – The Witches Sabbat	Mastery of the Subconscious
6	Golab	Geburah - Mars	Grade II – The Witches Sabbat	Transformation of self into individual, separate consciousness
5	Togaririm	Tipheret – Black Sun	Grade I – Blackened Forge of Cain	The True Will Emerging
4	Harab Serapel	Netzach - Venus	Grade I – Blackened Forge of Cain	Creation of the Mind, substantial results with Magick
3	Samael	Hod - Mercury	Grade I – Blackened Forge of Cain	Reawakening and establishment of Will
2	Gamaliel	Yesod - Moon	Grade 0 – Nahemoth And the Black Earth	Emotional control and discipline
1	Nehemoth and Lilith	Malkut - Earth	Grade 0 – Nahemoth And the Black Earth	Discipline And practice

Grade structure and the Qlippoth

The structure of TOPH within the Qlippoth is presented, however the Great Work itself is much more intense than presented in this simple diagram. Initiation via the Left Hand Path and Luciferian Magick challenges every aspect of your being, causing real life change and progression.

THE REALM OF THE QLIPPOTH

The Tree of Life and Death is as old as ancient Babylonia and Assyria. The subject of this study and the foundation of practice will be based around the Hebraic model of understanding. The Qlippoth is a work of mystery; it unfolds in each initiate and magickian who is able to wield the power contained therein. As one progresses through the realm of shades and daemonic energies the question of "I" will emerge. The sense of "who you are" will be a concept which shall be revealed over time and through effort. Often, inner or outer struggle will define this along with your application of the "Ritual of Azal'ucel" or a similar work focused on bringing the magickian directly in communion with ones' Daemon or Luciferic Angel.

It has been suggested by students such as Fuller that the philosophy of the Qabalah is about a return to balance as the state of the original Adam of the Jews. While this may be the aim of the traditional Right Hand Path initiate, the Left Hand Path or Luciferian will seek balance in the forbidden, often a place of great power which is concealed due to its potential destructive force. All things worth conquering will offer risk, as a Luciferian you must understand if this is worth your study and prospect into the mysteries of darkness.

Within the Qlippoth, the Realm of God is not that of the Hebraic God. It is the Samael, the beast or dragon which commands darkness and the chaos-realms of hell. The Luciferian can see the light hidden within this darkness, knowing this, a path towards mastery and self-deification is found through its transcendence.

The Ritual of "Casting the Circle of the Dragon" and the "Lesser Encircling Rite of the Luciferian" found in "The Bible of the

Adversary" will provide solid ritual foundations for the great work itself. Consider that these rites provide the proper flooring needed for this work, in order to ensure the aim is consistent with Luciferian aspirations. Understanding this, know that Luciferian invocations are callings to the self, the dragon to rise up from the depths as the bringer of light. With this said, there is no evil action nor negative approach. In the forbidden realms of darkness there is enlightenment and power for those brave and strong enough to reach forth and grasp these roots.

The word called "qlippah" or "klippah" (the plural being "qlippoth") means "shell" or "husk", such may be symbolized as a corpse or empty shell. The Magickian will fill these shells with a semblance of life from the atavistic depths of the mind, thus a type of necromancy. Once these shells have been activated with the Daemonic world, the energies associated may absorbed in the psyche.

The Signature of Lucifer, from a Medieval Pact

DEMONIC RULERS AND NAMES OF POWER

The names of the spiritual servitors of Qlippothic ArchDemons are symbolized as the name of the ruler. For example, Thamiel (Hebrew ThAMAL) is served by Abraxiel, Thadekiel, Mahaziel (Mahazael), Azazael (Azazel) and Lufugiel. The servitors of each Qlippothic order and sphere operate in the same manner. When invoking or evoking Qlippothic spheres, entering them and gaining knowledge of them you must recite and vibrate the names associated with the sphere.

The Qlippoth rule on earth in temporal form as they manifest in different ways and continually change their forms. For instance, Thamiel may be invoked to guide you in a leadership role. After a period of time, Thamiel will seemingly fade away in the manifestation in which it was called. Those working with Thamiel in a Vampyric way such as in the Order of Azariel will seek to devour and absorb the energy of the specific sphere in question, from which the energy remains with you in the mind.

The Qlippoth are made manifest in earth depending on how you conjure them. If you are seeking a working to gain a deeper knowledge of your Daemon or Genius, utilizing HOD will perhaps set in motion a serious of compelling instances in which you will gain the chance to initiate yourself into this communion. The Luciferian Adept may use Magick in this way – to compel that which is around you to lend support and command circumstances to change beneficially in your supporting manner.

ArchDemons rule the earth in a transcendent manner, meaning that much like the Daemon/Luciferian Angel/Holy Guardian Angel/Azal'ucel the spiritual manifestation of the Archdemons are invisible and instinctual.

THE NATURE OF MAGICKIAL ENERGY

The Ten Hells in Seven places are spheres of specific types of deific energy. These storehouses of power are indeed viable in the physical world. The Adept who wants to work with Qlippothic Spheres must utilize the foundation of Will + Desire + Belief. Austin Osman Spare described a potent method of sorcery in his workings surrounding sigils. Demonic energies, I describe "demonic" as their "Therionick" or primal attributes, are carefully connected to each specific Sphere and the 'type' of energy they represent.

For example, Malkuth and Yesod relate directly to the earth and moon, respectively. The Adept may invoke the Nahemoth for means of gaining the insight of others' and their relative desires. Having this knowledge will allow circumstances to fall in your favor in daily work or social life. Yesod relates to the Moon and the Qlippoth of Lilith will inspire sexual insight and lustful workings, not to mention the highly intuitive and emotional insight. This is how the "Alphabet of Desire" is rooted and created from. It is a literal compact and direct language of the subconscious which represents specific 'types' of power. This is exactly how the Qlippoth is separated and defined, areas or palaces of dark power and wisdom.

THE FOUNDATION OF THE WORK

The Adept shall if working within ceremonial settings shall focus on the work at hand the day of the operation. The attributes of the Qlippothic Palace shall be kept on mind and focused on during the course of the day prior to operation. Adepts may wish to perform the "Ritual of Azal'ucel" to invoke clarity the day of the work, allowing the psyche to focus on the working with more intensity once performed. It is suggested as with any workings of Goetia (howling), be it Luciferian Magick or Therionick Sorcery to align the Daemon with the Conscious Mind, to allow the potential for greater success in the work.

THE MAGICKAL INSTRUMENTS OF DARKSOME ART

The instruments are described in detail in works such as "Luciferian Witchcraft", "Luciferian Goetia" and "The Bible of the Adversary" among others however will be described in basic detail here. You should acquire or create such items prior towards operations if you are approaching in a ceremonial manner. If you are using this within an "Astral temple" or visualized setting, you may adapt using your imagination accordingly.

Invocation and Evocation (Invocation – calling within, Evocation – calling outside of the self) are processes which require the application of imagination and fully absorbing yourself in the work at hand. If you perform an invocation with little luster or concentration, don't expect suitable results.

THE CIRCLE

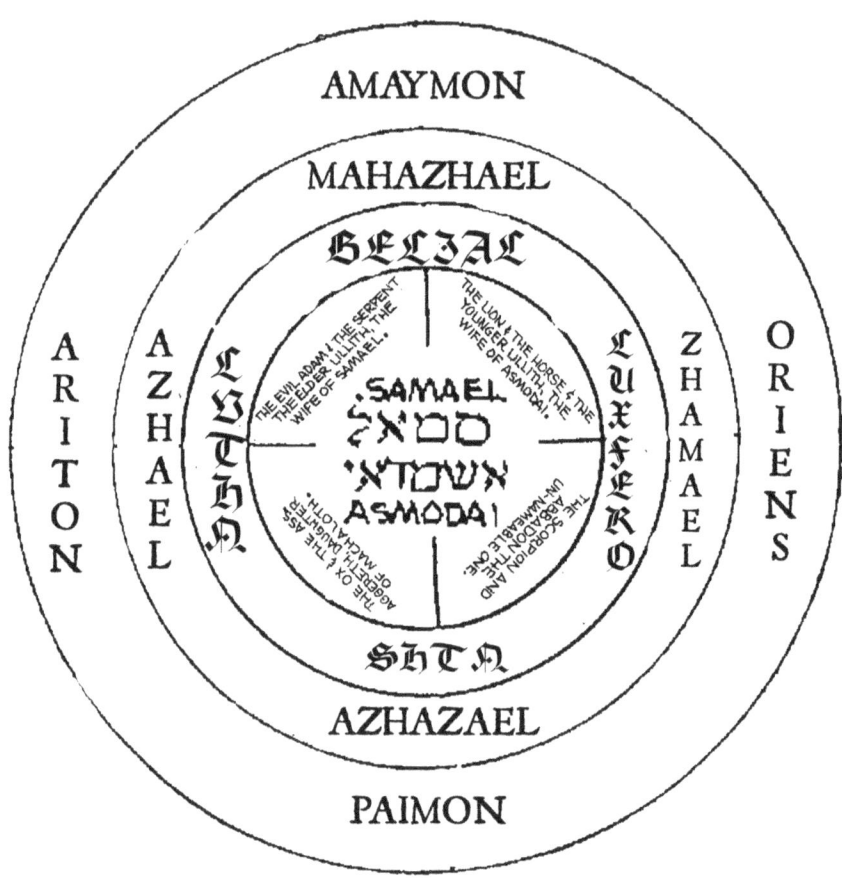

The Circle of the Adversary may be utilized. The proper definitions are given in "The Bible of the Adversary". The infernal names are specific types of power and no other types be used representing any "holy" or Judeo-Christian God commanding. The Circle is the circumference of the Adept, the very ensorcelling place of spirits wherein is the sacred crossroads of Luciferian Magick. The Qlippothic Archdemons mentioned in the circle are empowering forces, not fearful or destroying ones. The Adept should view them as a part of the self as even if they are perceived as independent "spiritual beings", they still must manifest in some way through you before a connection may be made. This is the foundation of the Luciferian motto of "There is no God but the Self" and is essential to the Luciferian ideology. This is why some Luciferians utilize and associate Leviathan as the symbol of the circle, representing the primal dragon of timeless being.

THE TRIANGLE

The Triangle is the focus point for spiritual energies, deific masks and spirits. The Triangle represents the Luciferian Trinity, the circle the Leviathanic foundation of timeless being. Outside of the circle instead of the Judeo-Christian "Angels" AZ-AZ-EL is written to encircle and empower the spiritual forces, to maintain the mental foundation or the Adept that the Luciferian is a part of the work constructed, that it is not only arrogant yet foolish to try and compel something without fleshly life to conduct according to our Will.

THE WAND

The wand has long been suggested to be composed of cedar or rosewood however I have discovered through personal experience you may use a human bone with a small crystal fitted in the end. Use any type of wand you feel "close" or connected to, it you may inscribe words ensure they are the words of power associated with the Luciferian path. At no time should a Christian name be used. The only alternative in this is TETRAGRAMMATON as the Luciferian symbolism is described with detail in "The Luciferian Goetia" and "Luciferian Witchcraft".

THE KNIFE

The handle of the blade if able to be burnt or inscribed should be AZAZEL or an associative name.

THE ROBE

Ceremonial workings may include a robe, which should be Black or a color fitting to your nature and the workings. You may have a sigil or symbol relating to the nature of the Luciferian Path upon it. Have no traditional "Judeo-Christian" God names or symbols upon it, else you curse your work before even beginning.

THE INCENSES:

Myrrh, Asafetida, Skullcap, Wolf's Bane, Yew, Morning Glory, Cypress - **Saturn**
Saffron, Dandelion, Chestnut, Clove, Nutmeg, Witch Grass - **Jupiter**
Sulfur, Damiana, Dragon's Blood, Wormwood (associated with Samael in Mars) - **Mars**
Gum Arabic, Cinnamon, Frankincense, Lime, Oak, Sandlewood - **Sol**
Mugwort, Rose, Valerian, Vanilla, Lilac - **Venus**
Mandrake, Almond, Clover, Lavendar, Mulberry - **Mercury**
Jasmine, Myrrh, Sandalwood, Wormwood (associated with Lilith) - **Moon**
Mugwort, Horehound, Cypress, Patchouly, **Earth**

PART TWO:
INVOCATIONS

LUCIFERIAN TRINITY INVOCATION

A simplistic and effective "banishing" or mind-clearing rite, the Luciferian Trinity invocation may be used before and after Qlippothic workings.

Visualize three forces at your feet, empowering you and lifting you upward while envisioning them while reciting their names:

RAHAB! *(whose symbol is a terrible demon leaping upon an Ox or appears as the Leviathan Serpent-Dragon with burning eyes)*

MACHALOTH! *(a form compounded of a serpent and a woman, and she rides upon a serpent scorpion)*

LILITH! *(a woman outwardly beautiful but inwardly corrupt and putrefying, riding upon a strange and terrible beast)*

The force which they encircle around you is a blackened-fire enshrouded whirlwind.

Visualize a Great Blackened Fire above your head:

SAM-AEL!

Visualize a great fiery serpent, black in appearance which rises up from the earth through you until it reaches your head:

ISHETH-ZENUNIM!

Take your hands and touch your chest, visualizing a beast or dragon rising from the sea from the union of the Infernal Couple:

CHI-OA!

Once you have recited this, clear your mind of all things at once.

SUMMONING THE SPIRITS OF THE QLIPPOTH

Calling the Spirits of the Qlippoth may be done by creating a symbol or sigil (using one from a previous source) and placing it within the Azazel Triangle. If you do this via the Astral temple, simply visualize a very basic sigil which is easy to mentally "see". You may use Goetic invocations or one printed in "The Bible of the Adversary". The adept may cause them to visualize in some form or feed their energy therein by offering blood or sexual fluid. If it is to be blood, it should be your own that there is a bonding element cast therein. The Spirits will feed from this blood until the energy from it is dissolved, yet they will still be connected to you. You may call forth the QLIPPOTHIC DEMONS without a place prepared for them, using simply visualization techniques or if you feel better about it, the AZAZEL triangle.

Some Black Adepts of the Black Order of the Dragon and Order of Azariel consuming the spiritual energy conjured in the triangle, entering and devouring it as Aapep would the Sun. This act of predatory spiritualism will fully activate your initiation and fuel the path itself.

THE FALLEN ANGELICK CONJURATION

I conjure thee forth, witness and gather to me

O most illustrious Prince of Heavenly and Abyssic Host

My angel of self-illumination AZAZEL – SAMAEL – BELIAL – RAHAB

The Watchers, the Nephilim gather from thy darkened palaces and envenom my workings! Empower me through my Mind, Spirit and Body to ascend the Throne of Satan's path!

O Unholy Angels, who have balanced darkness and bear light

Who gather serpents and the beasts of the earth

With whom shades of the dead gather, Come forth!

To the Great Red Dragon which brought forth Life on Earth

Who keeps the Abode of Witches and Sorcerer's full of Wisdom

Whose twenty-two scales are as biting shields against the profane!

Hail thou Adversarial Blackened Dragon, whose eyes are as great torches!

Send thy Black Archangels to me that we may expand our Will in this world! Let them come forth to me that my own strength, wisdom and desire in this world shall be sated!

Bring strength unto me and through me, My Daemon, by thy Great Angel Belial, who is the rebellious spirit of strength and cunning insight, to you Lucifer, who smashes down the weakened slave-angels of a lackluster power! Who reigns in Hell and resides again in his own created Heaven, Hail Adversary! AZOTHOZ!

Leviathan by Dore

QLIPPOTIC PRAYERS
By Dualkarnain

These Prayers of the Qlippoth contain a recital to occur in the morning and one in the evening in accordance with the sleep cycles of the Initiate.

These Prayers are to be recited upon awakening each morning or evening, according to the sleep cycles of the Initiate. They must occur before any other action is taken, even urination. Begin with the first Prayer of Nahema. Recite it daily until it has been memorized fully. Once perfectly executed in the morning and evening for the first time, continue this prayer for 3 days.

Practice it throughout the day if you wish to memorize the prayer as this will expedite the entire process. While the rhymes appear trite and simple, their meaning astrally etches the Initiate sufficiently and without dross.

THE QLIPPOTH

The Qlippoth or Qlipoth is the Hebrew realm of shells, or the dark, averse Tree of Life. While most Cabalists hold contempt and fear for the Tree of Death, the able Luciferian who is able to consciously (and subconsciously) enter the realm of the Adversary may grow strong from the dark current. From a Left Hand Path perspective, the Qlippoth is a powerful source of primal wisdom, it is a current which feeds the depths of the mind and spirit. The Luciferian who may tap into this "darkness", will gain empowerment from the daemonic forces and the shadows therein.

The Averse Sephiroth is called unclean, as it is not of the world of the so-called "God". The Tree of Death or Da'ath (hidden knowledge, wisdom) is ensorcelled by the rays of the Coils of the Crooked Dragon.

There are eleven classes within the Qlippoth, however they are called ten.

TEN HELLS IN SEVEN PLACES

Shahul-
The Grave Hell of the Supernals, The Triple Hell

Abaddon-
Perdition

Tythihoz-
Clay of Death

Barashechath-
The Pit of Destruction

Tzalemoth-
The Shadow of Death

Sha'arimrath-
The Gates of Hell

Giyehanim-
Hell

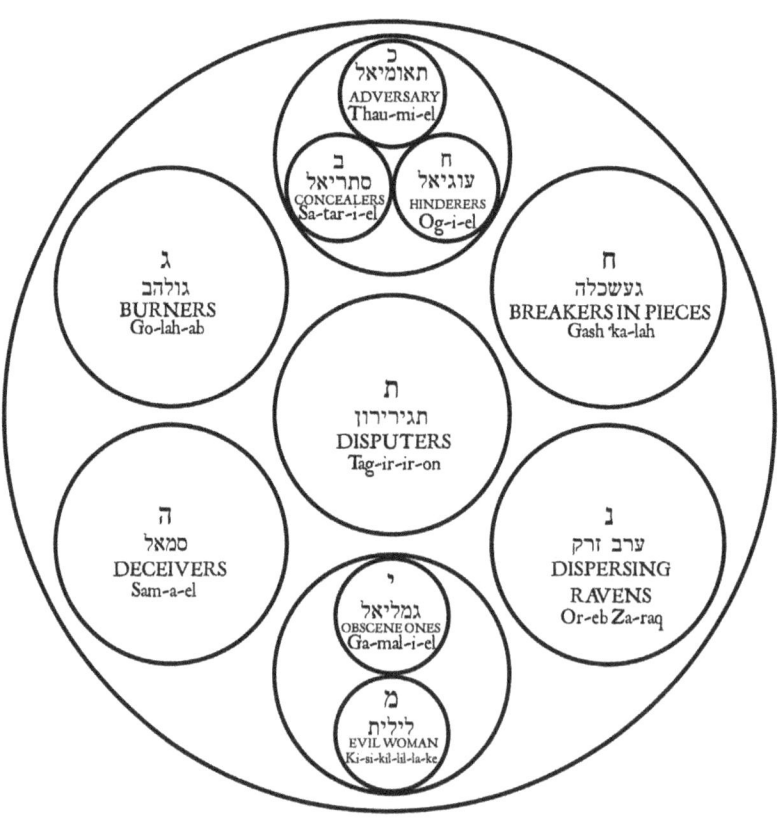

There are seven heads of this ancient dragon yet once the Luciferian gain power and wisdom within it, an eighth head arises. There are seven infernal palaces in which the Daemonic Gods sit upon their Thrones, yet they do include ten.

Leviathan, an ancient and powerful symbol of initiation and strength presents a strong foundation to the Qlippoth and the Great Work therein. Leviathan was known as the Akkadian Mus-Sag-Imin, a seven headed dragon and Lord of Chaos, Lotan was the name of Leviathan when he battled with Baal.

Leviathan is described in Job xli. 18: "By his neesings a light doth shine, and his eyes are like the eyelids of the morning". Leviathan is thus the empowering one, the very Dragon which beholds the power of the circle and timeless being. This is why many view Leviathan as the symbol of Ourabouris, or primal chaos as the circle itself.

Signature of Leviathan from a Medieval pact.

TRANSITIONING THROUGH THE DARK PALACES

Working with Qlippothic demons and forces of chaos by definition will challenge the Adept who seeks such forbidden knowledge. Approach is imperative to such operations, however. If you approach the Qlippoth in a bullying, overbearing way trying to command the name of the Judeo-Christian or Cabalistic "God" then expect just what they warn you about – madness, chaos, death or failure. If you approach the Qlippoth as a Luciferian; seeking wisdom, balanced and approaching as a Brother or Sister, a "child" the Samael and Lilith then you will be empowered and charged with their power and wisdom. Once you gain this, however, be careful not to lose your sense of balance and direction, for often it grows easy to fall into this trap.

Invoke the dark spheres with the Prayers and Words of Power; you may use sigils which hold direct meaning and others elsewhere such as in "AKHKHARU". Start with Malkuth, when summoning forth the power of these specific "hells" or "hidden places of power" you will call forth and compel through the prayers, aligning your conscious and subconscious mind, then with the Names of Power, Barbarous names of the demonic forces bringing forth the attributes of the spheres they emerge from. For instance, gaining a new place to live or expanding a relationship to benefit your goals Malkuth is a perfect place to begin. If you hunger for more, calling forth Gamaliel and visualizing what they represent and appearance will trigger a specific perception in your subconscious. In doing this, the demonic powers have granted a foundation to manifest. You will see your approach in work improve and more strategically conduct yourself which improves favor among those in power. Over a period of time, if you remain balanced and focused; circumstances will align to your Will and benefit you directly.

You may wish to have the Names of Power written down simply and focus on each day, remembering and activating their purpose and presence. You will then subconscious "act" towards supporting and then compelling things to essentially "go your way".

OF THE NAMES AND THEIR SYMBOLS

Keep it very simple and to the point. Depending on which Dark Palace or Qlippothic Sphere you are working with, you may wish to acquire or construct items or things reminding you of the specific demons and the powers they represent. Keep a clear mind is important, thus utilizing the Luciferian Trinity Invocation or another banishing/focus ritual is essential to remain clear towards your goals.

There are several rituals which utilizes the Barbarous Names of the Qlippothic demons in workings of empowerment. In "The Bible of the Adversary", the ritual "To Therion To anabainon ek Tes Abyssou" or "The Beast Rising from the Abyss" is a ritual of empowerment of the Mind – Spirit – Body of the Adept using infernal powers. The Magickian uses the names during the course to the ritual to empower the subconscious with activating elements of the brain in accordance to their attributes, thus allowing and compelling the demonic energy a gateway through the mind itself.

PART THREE:
THE QLIPPOTH
AND
TREE OF DA'ATH

MALKUTH – EARTH – NAHEMOTH

Within the earth does the Adept begin, the very passions of the mind and body will be brought under control and the Luciferian begin the empowerment of his or her Will. The Palace of Darkness which contains Malkuth and Yesod enthrones the demons called the Gamaliel, who are described as blood drinking and obscene bull-men. Kenneth Grant described the Gamaliel as being of Chaldean origin, that they are related to the dark side of the moon. Within the sphere of Malkuth does Lilith reign and empowers Nahemoth. The Moon of vampirism, the blood moon is symbolized as a crescent moon, horned and upward representing the desire to devour the higher gods.

This is the Seventh Palace or Hell which contains Yesod and Malkuth. Along with the Gamaliel are also referred Nachashiel, Evil Serpents, and Obriel. Thereunto belongeth the Blind Dragon-force, the Leviathanic principle which unites Samael and Lilith to create Baphomet or Chioa. Unto Malkuth is attributed Lilith, the Evil Woman of Darkest Desires, afterwards changing to a black, monkey-like demon.

The Black Adept may enter Malkuth by reciting the Demons of Earth, represented by Nahemoth, the demon of impurity. Grade 0 – Nahemoth and the Black Earth is a period of intense discipline and growing comfortable with magickal workings from a Luciferian perspective.

The Black Adept should utilize the Nahemoth and the Black Earth sphere to gain a perception of where you wish to go, thus a chaos inspired moment of continual self-creation.

PRAYER OF NAHEMOTH

All I wish, all I desire,
Whispering, burning fire.
Nahemoth keep me, longing thus
Heated calls of endless lust

By dust, desire, fire and gasp
I close this day in hunger-rasp
I thank you, now, Nahemoth
My heart, my mind, my heat my lust

RECITE THE NAMES OF POWER:

NAHEMOTH (NHMATh):
NOBREXIEL + HETERIEL + MOLIDIEL + A'AINIEL + THAUHEDRIEL

Using a black mirror or object of divination, you may visualize your desires found in earth, challenges in relationships, habits which lead to problems, etc. Open the gates to the kingdom of Gehenna with a pure heart and mind focused upon the task at hand.

You may find and empower these spirits according to your desires in the Earth, simply visualize them and focus on them as you think of your problem or challenge at hand. In Malkuth Lilith also may appear as a beautiful woman and then changing to a monkey-like demon. She is the bestial and Therionick power of lust and desire.

YESOD – MOON – Gamaliel

Herein is the Abode of Lilith, as previously mentioned within the Dark Palace the Gamaliel, the Obscene Ones and Vampiric spirits. The Dragon has illuminated Malkuth and Yesod in this palace and the Adept must gain the perception of how they will apply the attributes of this dark realm in the physical world.

If one grows distraught or confused in the realm, overcome with emotion you may gain control by visualizing a great Blackend Fire and then blinding light while invoking the Luciferian Trinity.

The words of power and entry into Yesod is:

PRAYER OF GAMALIEL

Of your dark contraband
Give me visions by your hand
Morning-blind, the moon did steal
Open my eyes, Gamaliel

Grateful I am as the moon now weeps
Through blistered visions I now sleep
Gamaliel, the day now closed,
Visions as you did propose.

***RECITE THE NAMES OF POWER** (calling them forth by repeating the names over and over again):*

GAMALIEL (GMLIAL):
GEDEBRIEL + MATERIEL + LAPREZIEL + IDEXRIEL + ALEPHRIEL + LABRAEZIEL

Some TOPH initiates (specifically female) utilize the Daughters of Lilith to expand their understanding of the Daemonic feminine and the Lunar Current. So many left hand path orders fail to understand the significance of the Female in terms of initiation and that Lilith is one half of the Adversary, the Bride of Samael.

HOD – MERCURY – Samael

The Sphere of HOD is associated with Mercury, transformation. Hod is the Qlippothic realm of continual advancement and progression, Samael the Adversary represents the Orders of the Demons here, who may be called upon to focus towards specific goals.

The Sixth Palace contains Hod, whereunto are referred the Samael or Deceivers, whose form is that of Demon-headed, dog/wolf-like monsters which are continually hungering. A glimpse of the Daemon or Initiatic/Luciferic Angel may be communed with here. Workings of "Azal'ucel" to gain insight are useful in areas such as this.

Invoke Adramalech, the Lord of Blackened Fire with the following words:

PRAYER OF SAMAEL

By your anger, let me sprawl
Samael, let my skin crawl
Sticky sickness paths ensue
Of knowledge where I might intrude

Samael, you broke and killed
As you churned the great death-still
The day is done, your song is done
Hail to you, the Black Archon

RECITE THE NAMES OF POWER (calling them forth by repeating the names over and over again):

SAMAEL (SMAL):
SHEOLIEL + MOLEBRIEL + AFLUXRIEL + LIBRIDIEL

NETZACH – Venus – HARAB-SERAPEL

The Ravens of death are the encirclers or dispersing ravens, these are demon-headed ravens that rise up from a volcano. These are the demons which serve the creation of the mind and will, they are directly associated with BAAL, the God of the World worshipped in ancient times throughout the Middle East.

PRAYER OF HARAB SERAPEL

Let me feel the end of hell,
And start the whip, Harab Serapel
Wake me up and with me stay
Disturb the waters of this day

Thanking you, down I wind
No more have I, stagnant mind.
Awakened by your noisome knell
Here I praise, Harab Serapel.

***RECITE THE NAMES OF POWER** (calling them forth by repeating the names over and over again):*

**HARAB-SERAPEL (HRB-SRRAL):
HELEBRIEL + RETERIEL + BARUCHIEL +
SATORIEL + REFREZIEL + REPTORIEL +
ASTORIEL + LABREZIEL**

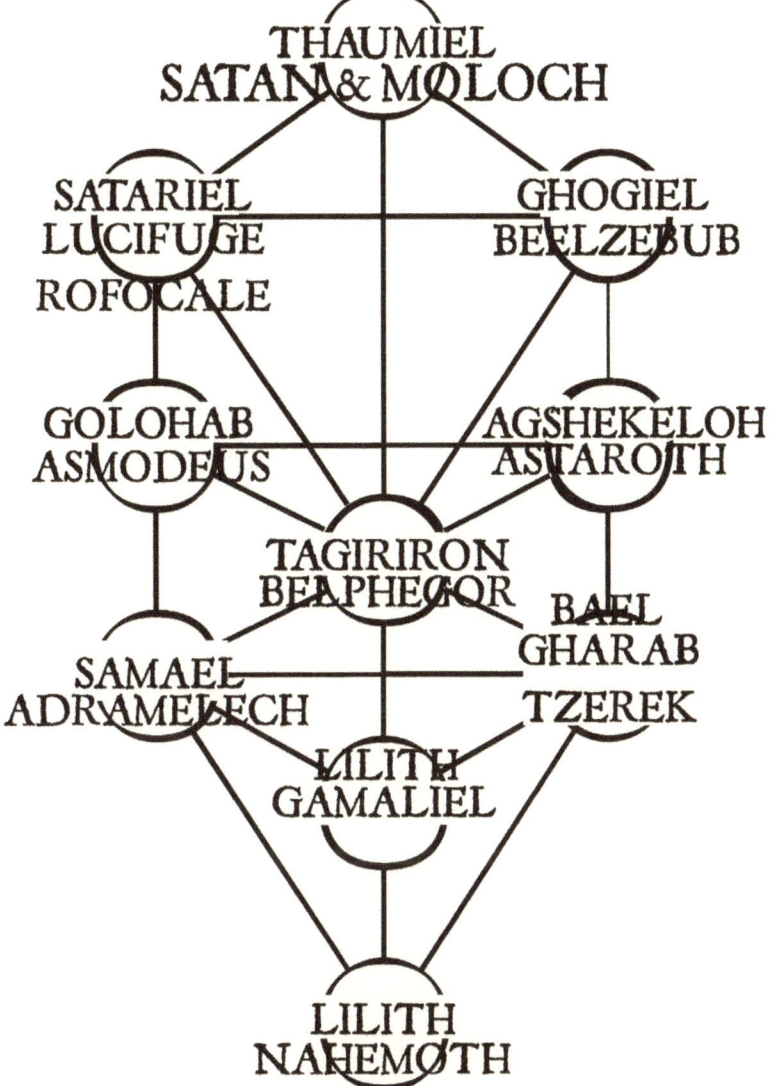

The Qlippoth and Tree of Da'ath

TIPHERETH – SUN – TAGARIRIM

A very powerful sphere related to the Sun, or within Qlippothic considerations the Black Sun. The Tagaririm rule this sphere and are related to the creative energies of darkness. The Black Sun of Belphagor has found attribution to the realm of the dead, rather the empowering of shades as well. Belphagor is the "Lord of Opening" is initiates one to the power of Tagaririm and Tiphereth, the Black Sun. Belphagor in traditional demonology is a demon of discoveries and inventions.

The Fourth Palace contains Tiphereth which are attributed Zamiel, and they are great black giants or Nephilim who are the children of the Daughters of Cain and the Watchers, or Luciferian Angels called the Grigori.

PRAYER OF BELPHAGOR

In the heat of the Burning Black Sun
With the spark of light against the spirit core
Illuminate me Belphagor
With thy angels of Tagaririm

Bring me the knowledge of my Daimon
That rapture is the invention
ZOMIEL, thou revolt of God
Belphagor smile upon my designs

Invoke the Tagaririm (Disputers) by reciting the names of their Tribes:

RECITE THE NAMES OF POWER (calling them forth by repeating the names over and over again):

TAGARIRIM (TGRRM): TAUMESHRIEL + GOBRAZIEL + RAQUEZIEL + REBREQUEL + MEPHISOPHIEL

GEBURAH – MARS – GOLAB

The Sphere of Geburah is related to "the left arm" or specifically the left axis. This sphere is ideal in initiatory aims as it relates to Might and Power. Asmodeus is the demon prince of this sphere. Mars itself is the God of War; in all cultures has a strong manifestation of violence. Aeshma is the daeva or Persian spirit of the wounding spear or bloody mace. Aeshma is the primal and ancient spirit of conquering and conflict, a primary Luciferian trait. Invoke Golab as the Spirit of the Raging Fiend, or primal lust and the drive to conquer any problem in your life. Often the struggle and Will assists in the "forge" aspect of initiation.

The Third Palace contains Geburah whereunto are attributed Golaheb, or Burners with Fire, being essentially the Black Flame and are otherwise called Zaphiel, and their forms are those of enormous black heads like avolcano in eruption. This powers are warlike and hungering in their nature. Many of the powers of Mars are held long with memories of ancient Assyria, Persia and other areas of primal, warlike history.

PRAYER OF GOLAB

Aeshmadeva thou spear wielding archfiend
Who inspires and brings violent strength
May I conquer and rend asunder my enemies
My spear to taste the blood of my offerings

Golab, burning ones of fortitude
I invoke your strength and violence
By the left arm I wield the power
To strike down those in my way

Power of blackened fire
To Will my spirit beyond fleshly death
In offerings to fire I have met
Golab, Asmodeus bless me in thy Light!

***RECITE THE NAMES OF POWER** (calling them forth by repeating the names over and over again):*

GALEB (GLEB): GAMELIEL + LEBREXIEL + EBAIKIEL + BARASHIEL

CHESED – GAMECHICOTH – ASHTAROTH

We now come to Chesed, the idea and an offering of substance to lower forms. The Wisdom of the Predatory spirit, the Azariel and Gamchicoth, the "Devourerers" are present in this sphere. The binding or ensorcelling ones may control and hold creative energy which the Adept may access and use via the sphere of Chesed. Jupiter is the sphere of Chesed and related to a source of divinity and creation. Let the Adept seek to take the cup of self-divinity and gain the creative elixir of birth and spiritual reinvigoration.

The Second Palace contains Chesed, unto which are attributed the Gagh Shekelah, the Disturbing Ones, and their symbolic forms are those of the black, cat-headed Giants. They are also called Aziel, Chazariel and Agniel. Being devouring spiritual forces, the Adept may gain strength from them accordingly.

PRAYER OF AZARIEL – GAMCHICOTH

Bless my desire and creation
O binding ones of the subtle shadow
Who offer a cup of hell broth
To the lips of the dead
Let me drink deep of creation
And the essence of love
That I may tear into the heart of life
And flow through the veins of immortality

RECITE THE NAMES OF POWER (calling them forth by repeating the names over and over again):

**GAMEHIOTH (GAMChATh):
GABEDRIEL + AMDEBRIEL + MALEXIEL +
CHEDEBRIEL + A'OTHIEL + THERIEL**

DAATH – CORONZON

Herein is the hidden darkness of Da'ath, the hidden place of infernal wisdom. This is the Gate of the Abyss, the place of eternal darkness yet also transformation. The Adept who enters Da'ath holds the key to the power of illumination, as the Black Flame or Consciousness is the Luciferic Torch which shapes the darkness to the Will. Coronzon is the Guardian of the Abyss. Coronzon is regarded as Samael, the Adversarial Light Bringer who also poisons the weak ones. Coronzon or Choronzon guards the wisdom of the Tree of Darkness, thus within the so-called Hell is self-empowerment and desire. Da'ath is the hidden palace of darkness wherein the Eighth Head of the Dragon resides; the Angel Samael whose number is 131 descends as the Wisdom of the Adept called the Azal'ucel or Daemon of Will.

Da'ath is the power of intellect in creation; it is the place of the "Hidden God" or Luciferian Daemon or Angel. The 8th Head which emerges is corresponding to the 8 points of Algol or the Black Sun Sigil. Kenneth Grant made reference to A.E. Waite in "The Holy Kabbalah, book X" from Medieval Qabalistic Pico della Mirandola that "The letters of the name of the evil demon who is the prince of this world (i.e. Set, Satan) are the same as those of the name of God, Tetragram, and he who knows how to effect their transposition can extract one from the other".

Crossing into Da'ath is often accompanied with a major life-shaking event such as a period of struggle and seeming (at that moment) desolation and hopelessness. The Adept will soon find the spirit or Daemon which invigorates him and allows expansion of consciousness. Coronzon is feared by Qabalists and Magickians as being a complete devouring demon. While Coronzon is a Vampiric manifestation of Samael, it is the primal or hungering aspect which seeks continued existence and the power of spirit. Coronzon may guide the initiate accordingly. The Priesthood of The Order of Phosphorus are involved in Coronzon workings at an early stage of their individual transformation.

Workings with Da'ath may be conducted during periods of extreme personal duress and struggle. You should keep a diary of the details of this time period so you may reflect upon it later. Consider that if you are conducting Qlippothic Workings, you may seek it during a period with the following Prayer, to keep a focus towards the wisdom which falls here.

It is the Dual-Headed Beast which Kenneth Grant calls Choronzon-Shugal (333 + 333) in Nightside of Eden which presents the Adversarial Power as one of initiation. From the Typhonian Current one may view the Luciferian Trinity as falling in place with this Dual Headed Beast as well, offering a cup to those willing to drink from it.

PRAYER OF DA'ATH

ZAZAS, ZAZAS, NASATANADA ZAZAS
Shadow substance gateway of hell
I seek thou infernal spell
To rip and rend against the face of God
To gain immortal consciousness above
Guide me Old Dragon thou Serpent Soul
Mighty Coronzon father and Devil
That wisdom is brought down in blinding light
Illuminated by the crown of the serpent-lion

BINAH – SATAHARIEL – LUCIFUGE

Binah, the Sphere of Concealed perfection, is the sphere of the Adept illuminated, emerged and empowered as isolate consciousness. Sathariel is the ones who hide perfection or self-deification, they don't keep it from the Adept, and rather they hide it simply from those unwilling to "see" it, thus a focus on perception. Once you have passed through Da'ath your vision will be aligned to gain the gift of Deification from Satherial/Satahariel and Lucifuge, the Shadow-Demon King of this sphere. The Sheireil or "Hairy ones" are Therionick or Beast-like shades which fuel the atavistic desires of the Adept.

Medieval grimoires traditions describe Lucifuge and Mephistopheles as soul-dragging pact makers, wherein this is only the situation if one approaches them with the Judeo-Christian or traditional Qabalah paradigms. If one enters as a Luciferian Adept, the viewpoint is consistently different and the result will be greater therein.

Lucifuge Rofocale is the King of the Sphere of Binah. Lucifuge, a name meaning "fly against the light" represents his power within darkness. Lucifuge is given the power by Lucifer over the treasures of the earth. Treasures of the earth relate to the wisdom and power of the

Adept. Thus the power within Binah is "Understanding" and is symbolized as well by Baphomet, thus the "Father of Understanding".

The Qlippoth of Binah are referred the Satariel / Harasiel, being the Concealers and Destroyers whose appear as gigantic, veiled Head with horns and hideous burning eyes seen through the veil of darkness. The Satariel are followed by centaurs. These are also called Seriel from Esau, because of their hairiness or Therionick manifestations.

Lucifuge Rofocale

PRAYER OF LUCIFUGE

Hail He who flies the light
Who resides upon earth as a king of wisdom
I seek the treasure not of false gold
Yet the gold of wisdom refined
Unto thou Luciferic Angel I call
Rise with me and show me sights
Of infernal and earthly delight
Sataral shadows with me

RECITE THE NAMES OF POWER (calling them forth by repeating the names over and over again):
SATERIEL (SATARAL):
SATURNIEL + ABNEXIEL + TAGARIEL + ASTERIEL + REQRAZIEL + ABHOLZIEL + LAREZIEL

CHOKMAH – CHAIGIDEL – BEELZEBUB

Chokmah, the first power of conscious intellect with creation is a direct manifestation of the Will and intellect, the Black Flame within human consciousness. The important note within Chokmah is that the ZODIACK and Tribes of the Qlippoth may be found through this level, as the planets and constellations are often said to be expressions of the Adversarial Spirit.

The orders of demons called Chaigidel are "hinderers" and those which breed adversity to those unable to comprehend their true nature. Concealed initiation is the nature of self-evolution and the Daemon or Luciferian Angel.

"Those who go forth into the empty place of God", the very nature of antinomianism is the essence of this sphere. Beelzebub is the ArchDemon of Chokmah and brings Adversarial Light to Adam Belial, a grotesque skeletal form of Chokmah.

The Qlippoth of Chokmah are referred the Dukes of Esau and the Ghogiel (from Og, King of Bashan) and Oghiel, and they attach themselves unto living and material appearances, and their form is like that of the black, evil Giants with loathsome serpents coiled around them.

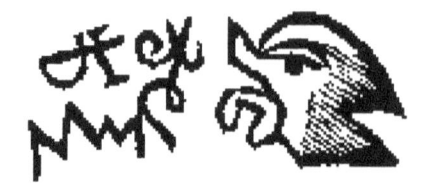

PRAYER OF BEELZEBUB

My prayer I offer
ArchDemon of flies and darkness
Beelzebub thou Spirit of Old
Fill me with pestilence
That my Palace empty of God
Has offered me a throne of my own making
Hinder and restrain my enemies
Fill me with the strength they waste against you
Ogiel I call to thee!

RECITE THE NAMES OF POWER (calling them forth by repeating the names over and over again):

CHAIGIDEL (ChIGDAL):
CHEDEZIEL + ITQUEZIEL + GOLEBRIEL + DUBRIEL + ALHAZIEL + LUFEXIEL

KETHER – THAMIEL – SATAN & MOLOCH

Kether is the sphere of Adversarial Enlightenment, of darkness absolute. Yet within the veil of darkness is the Black Flame of Light, the Will triumphant. The wisdom of Thamiel is the perception of the power of the Adversary.

Thamiel is the Adversarial Power of the focused mind; the one who is in perfect communion with his or her "Daemon" or Genius. Thamiel are revolted aspects of higher articulation, they are "fallen angels" or Adversarial Spirits which breed not only emotions of spiritual dissent yet also the intellect to command them. Moloch, one of the dual or Adversarial Gods of this sphere is one of the oldest manifestations of the Luciferian spirit, one which ancient Hebrews and other peoples sacrificed "seed" to in his fires.

To "Pass through the Fire to Moloch" in Luciferian perspective is to pass through the Blackened Flame of Consciousness, initiation and the realization of your place and destiny in this world. Kether is the Adversarial Mind, the place where dissent has made one absolute and "God" in terms of who you are.

The Two Giant Heads with Bat-like wings represent the Adversarial Shadow and predatory nature relating to the subconscious mind. The Qlippoth of Kether are the Bicephalous ones (Thaumiel); and as their forms are those of dual, giant heads, with bat-like wings; they do not have bodies for they are those who seek continually to unite themselves unto the bodies of other beings and forces. Thamiel are powerful vampiric or predatory demons which may be used in various ways by the Adept who may channel them accordingly.

Those who work with Kether in Qlippothic workings will seek only communion with "Azal'ucel" has been made, the True Will or Daemon is essential in this level of spiritual initiation. The Adversarial Spirit in Kether is the yearning and lust for more in life, when nothing is ever good "enough" and balance must continually be sought. Those who do not approach Kether and Thaumiel/Thamiel correctly with this discipline will cause their own mind and thus life to ruin and pain.

PRAYER TO THAUMIEL

By the drums of Topheth Sound
By the Fires of Moloch unbound
I seek your Adversarial strength
Nightborn Thaumiel who fly the light
Upon the wings of bats
By the gift of Azazel given, shadow'd
Satan bless my work of highest reach
That I may ascend and fall as God enthroned
Alone and powerful unto my own
I shall pass through the Fire to you Moloch

***RECITE THE NAMES OF POWER** (calling them forth by repeating the names over and over again)*:

**THAMIEL (ThAMAL):
THADEKIEL + ABRAXSIEL + MAHAZIEL +
AZAZAèL +LUFUGIEL**

THE CROWN OF GODS, THE DEVIL QEMETIEL ABOVE KETHER

Qemetiel is the very Crown of the Gods, the Devil who appears as a vast black, man-headed Dragon Serpent, the power of this Archon is to unite the force of Keth and the Infernal and Averse Sephiroth. Belial, the Power which denies all Gods and A'Athiel, which is uncertainty in the path of weakness. The three here are ABOVE the Qlippothic Kether and channels the manifestations in which it forms throughout the Tree of Death. The Black Adept should view Qemetiel as a powerful focus source of wisdom, thus meditating on the state of your current point of initiation.

Initiates should in their own good time go back to the lower spheres of the Qlippoth and experience workings with the demons once this contact has been achieved.

Qemetiel-
Crown of Gods, First Devil
The first is Qematriel, whose appear of a vast black, man-headed Dragon-serpent, and this power united under him the force of Kether of the Infernal and averse Sephiroth.

Belia'al-
The Power which denies all Gods, Wickedness.

GOTHIEL - A'Athiel
Uncertainty. Called also Othiel and Gothiel, appearing as a black, bloated Man-insect, horrible of every aspect, he unites the force of the averse Binah.

PRAYER TO THE CROWN OF GODS

Qemetiel be as my Heilos of darkness
Wherein Black Flame illuminates the Mind
Qemetiel blackened serpent coil
To whisper knowledge in hissing tones
Belial my father who denies all Gods
Keep me focused upon my path
That through Gothiel I shall always seek self-excellence
Wisdom, power and immortality of my mind
Samael the Black, crown may work with your wisdom!

PART FOUR: THE ZODIACK OF THE QLIPPOTH

THE ZODIACK OF THE QLIPPOTH

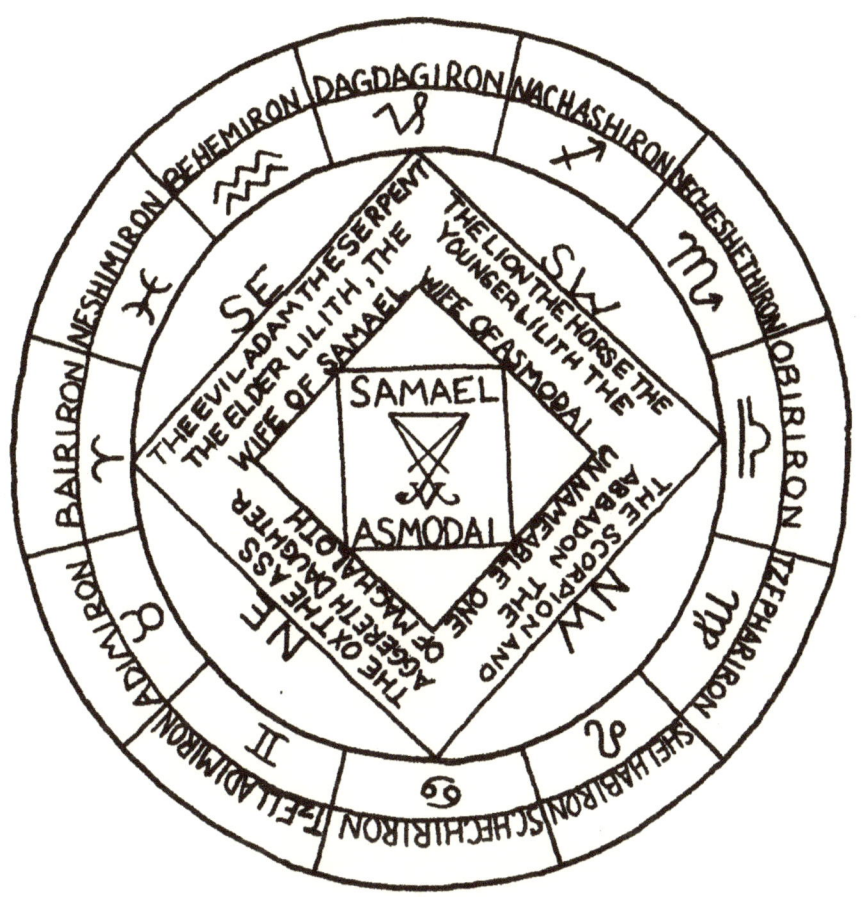

The Zodiac of the Qlippoth (spelled also 'Zodiack') is the nightside which holds tribes of demons which are able to enter and exert influence in this world according to the time in which they are associated. The Order of Phosphorus initiate should remain focused and consider this with the symbol above. Samael / Asmodai representing the Black Adept as the vessel of the Deific mask. Grade 0 of Nahemoth and the Black Earth is exclusively about structure and discipline. This should be always be the centering point of your workings. The pillars of the Adversary – ending with Abaddon are supporting forces of initiation. Remember that the Adversarial current is about strength and power.

Capricorn (Dec.22 – Jan. 19) **Active Earth**

DAGDAGIRON – Manifests in the form of devouring fish, color – Red. Represents leadership, strength, ambition and materialism. Use this sphere to align thought with the attributes of Dagdagiron. Capricorn is essentially ruled by the Planet Saturn, often associated with the astrological tenth house.

Invoking the Dagdagiron during this time period with traditional invocations will provide the Black Adept with some foundation. What should be considered is that specific symbolism – the sign of Capricorn or the gateway of the Dagdagiron should be kept near you during this time period. Capricorns most are considered practical, ambitious, disciplined and careful. Use this time to focus on your goals such as career or improving your relations in a similar area.

The Black Adept may invoke Dagdagiron during this period to focus on a singular goal to accomplish in a short period of time. The Ruling planet of Capricorn, Saturn is the Adversarial Planet; both octaves of Lucifer and Satanas in Saturn offer a balanced initiatory experience.

The Order of Phosphorus is centered on levels of initiation.

Aquarius (Jan. 20 – Feb.17) **Fixed Air**

BEHEMIRON – It is said the arms were derived from Behemoth, considered beasts in the form of Hippopotamus – Elephants with their skin spread flat like a cockroach. Color- black-brown.

The Behemiron are forms of Behemoth, a beast ridden by Satanas in medieval apocalyptic lore. The Black Adept working in Behemiron will seek to plan out some long term plans, something six months or beyond and step by step write it out.

The Behemiron are very useful in bringing forth nightmares about the future, you can seek wisdom in this way! Communication is an excellent point in working with Behemiron. Summon this Qlippothic force to learn and excel in communicating in groups or other people. Practice and keep a sigil of the demonic tribe when conducting workings to improve this.

Pisces (Feb. 18 – Mar. 19) **Mutable Water**

NESHIMIRON – Hideous demon women, skeleton like, united with the bodies of serpents. Color – watery blue

Inward emotion, introspection and the understanding of emotions – exploring emotions and learning to control them. Nocturnal desires, the daughters of Lilith born in her caves in Hell, wherein she creates and consumes life.

Explore your sexual desires, elements which pique your interest, seek to understand why. Use your hearing to observe the behaviors of others, learn to listen.

Watch their motions, their tone of voice – how do they sound, what are they really trying to say? When evoking or entering the sphere of Neshimiron, focus on the color of the demonesses. The Neshimiron will manifest in various mysteries in which you seek. The period of time around Pisces should prove useful in seeking to understand the self in a deeper way and what you want in terms of desire.

Aries (Mar. 20 – April 19) **Active Fire**

BAIRIRON – Dragon-Lion beast derived from Samael, color – black.

The Bairiron are fire demons who were given form by Samael, the Prince of the Fallen Angels. Bairiron are both darkness (air – dark matter) and Fire (air allows fire to be, to spread) these demons are active, violent in motion and very courageous. The Bairiron are guides of manifestation, of what you can achieve if you only try. They relate to the Warrior spirit, the conquering charge to accomplish what you wish.

A Luciferian symbol, Aries are fiery and self-liberated individuals. The Bairiron are daemonic powers which instill freedom and the determination or spirit to see something through.

The Bairiron are natural leaders and will either empower or cause breakdown in personality. The Black Adept must invoke them and control by meditation and focus the Qlippoth of Bairiron to utilize them properly. Ahrimanic Yoga will provide an excellent foundation for this.

Taurus (April 20 – May 20) Fixed Earth

ADIMIRON – Lion-Lizards color - yellow and gray. The Adimiron are very strong and determined demonic spirits, if the Black Adept conjures their presence during this period of time, it should be towards a focus in seeking to accomplish a challenge which has been lingering for a long period of time.

The Adimiron are a determined force, if invoked will provide a source of strength during a period of struggle or accomplishing something.

Gemini (May 21 – June 20) Mutable Air

TZELLADIMION – Savage and triangular headed dog like beasts, color – bronze and crimson. The Black Adept calling forth the Tzelladimion and very active demons, they may be called forth to observe two sides of a situation, to better learn how to play one against the other. That is the nature of Tzelladimion, to force the Adversarial Spirit to become very adaptable to situations and mastering them in a way which pleases everyone. This is one aspect of power which is often unrecognized in Luciferians.

Cancer (June 21 – July 22) **Active Water**

SCHECHIRIRON – reptile, insect and shellfish, demon faced. Color – black.

The Schechiriron are an aspect of the Moon, of Cancer and the emotion. These demons are found in the dreaming realm, swimming about the Goddess of the Moon and doing her bidding exclusively.

The Schechiriron may be summoned for drawing in close to the Dark Goddess, allowing her to inspire your ideas further.

Leo (July 23 – Aug 22) **Fixed Fire**

SHELHABIRON – Merciless and vicious wolves and jackals. Color, fiery yellow. These are aggressive and dominating powers, when working with the Shelhabiron your goals should be centered around accomplishing a task which requires near 'overkill' such as competing against a very strong enemy.

The Shelhabiron are also very creative, using such in a fire symbol will allow a great deal of imaginative spirits.

Virgo (Aug. 23 – Sept. 22) Mutable Earth

TZEPHARIRON – partially living yet decaying corpses, undead and shades in flesh. Color, earth.

The darkness found with the Tzephariron are Qlippothic forces which strip away exterior aspects and reveal the inner essence. Black Adepts who call forth the Tzephariron may use the Qlippoth to strip down all magickial operations to perceive what is essential and what is not.

Libra (Sept. 23 – October 22) **Active Air**

OBIRIRON – Gray bloated goblins, color – clouds. The Obiriron are the most balanced demonic shades of the Qlippoth as Libra is a traditional balanced sign. Workings with the Obiriron are very useful in workings of repose and carefully allowing a time of reasoning and understand your basis of initiation. Are you accomplishing your goals? Where are you failing? What did you learn which you can apply to your current workings?

Scorpio (Oct. 23 – Nov. 21) Fixed Water

NECHESHETHIRON – Devilish human headed insects, color, copper. The Qlippoth in Scorpio is a powerful mix of aggression and raw power, often tending towards destruction or rather changing of tides. The Necheshethiron may be worked with to keep focus towards change and your continual point of transformation.

Sagittarius (Nov. 22 – Dec. 21) Mutable Fire

NACHASHIRON – Dog headed serpents, colors of serpents. The Nachashiron are demons which tend to lead the Black Adept to the heart of the matter of their initiation. There are often specific elements of personality which cause a sense of struggle or tend to slow initiatory progress. The Nachashiron are force which inspire steady focus towards establishing Will and determined action. The Nachashiron are continually moving for purpose, fire. The Black Adept may seek to focus heavily on communion with ones' Daemon during this period, or manifesting a different level of initiation.

PART FIVE:
THE ORDER OF PHOSPHORUS

THE ORDER OF PHOSPHORUS

THEORY

Luciferianism is a philosophy centered on individuality and self-enlightenment. Often Luciferianism is misrepresented as being associated with devil-worship which could not be further from the truth. Lucifer is a symbol of enlightenment to Luciferians and not a literal being. While some believe in the existence of a literal "Adversary", a cosmic motivator who inspires evolution and chaotic growth, many Luciferians view the Adversary as a symbol or subconscious force of self-enlightenment and motivation, not a devil who wishes to damn humanity.

The Bible of the Adversary outlines various traditions of the Adversary throughout religion, mythology and magical initiatory systems which bring together the common elements of imagination (called in specific Islamic traditions as the essence of Iblis) and self-empowerment.

To understand Luciferianism as Michael W. Ford has defined it, one must look to early Enoch texts concerning the Watchers and Grigori. Until they "illuminated" humanity by teaching them the arts of magick and knowing the self, humans were thoughtless or selfless sheep. While the Judeo-Christian god calls this Serpent the "devil", the Adversarial spirit brought humanity the "Black Flame" or gift of individual consciousness.

The Luciferian embraces the Adversarial current in many forms, from a spiritual sense to those who have validated a "otherness" or "spirit world" as well as a physical sense, to those who cannot validate a "spirit world" and believe they exist in this world here and now with no thought towards an afterlife. Michael W. Ford understands that these two types of perceptions may be realized in a type of "Adversarial Chaos" which dictates no matter how you view the world or yourself, the mind and body must be shaped in this world as vessels of the Adversary, thus becoming living Gods accountable for their own destiny.

STRUCTURE AND PURPOSE

TOPH implements a left hand path initiatory style in the formulation of the grade structure. Beginning with entry into **Grade 0 – Nahemoth and the Black Earth**, TOPH initiates are instructed to gauge their experience with formal grade work, utilizing the Bible of the Adversary and other key works in formulating their individual perception of Luciferianism. This is the most difficult grade to grasp, initiates must think on how their "Judeo-Christian" foundations must be shaken off in exchange for a solid foundation of Luciferian thought. Instead of "conjuring demons" you are "empowering yourself". Every invocation is a calling of either a symbolic or spiritual force, what we call a "Deific Mask", of energy into the Temple that is the Mind – Body – Spirit. Every conscious and soon after subconscious act must be attuned towards self-evolution and self-enlightenment. Luciferians learn to balance "darkness" and "light" by "know thyself" and the application of Magick in self-creation. The Grade levels are deeply connected with the Qlippoth, wherein each level is directly attributed to the process of Magick you work through at that time.

Grade I – The Blackened Forge of Cain is a grade of the real essence of practice – here the Three Types of Luciferian Magick are practiced. Initiates discover that they are alone in their development, no matter who is around them! Self-accountability is a corner stone in the work of the Luciferian as he or she discovers their strengths and weaknesses through the application and practice of Luciferian Magick, the art of transforming the self into a Godlike Consciousness, through the darkness of the mind and spirit in Yatukih Sorcery, understanding primal atavisms and daemonic energies within and beyond the self and Therionick Sorcery, working with lower sorcery and understanding the animalistic aspects of the psyche.

The Daemon, Daimon, True Will or Luciferian Angel is sought in a work of chosen practice. "Azal'ucel" is the Perfect Daimon within each man and woman, the guiding instinctual force which makes us unique and powerful within the scope of our own life. This is a highlight of the Grade, a true mastery of the self!

It is within this grade that Adepts begin to explore their own chosen avenues of Luciferian Magick and apply them to their unique individuality.

Grade II – The Witches Sabbat is a state of being in which the Luciferian has successfully applied the path of Luciferianism and is considered an Adept of Algol. The Adept of Algol will work deeper into the Luciferian aspects of Magick and Sorcery, expanding at their own pace and desire through various inner orders and above.

INNER ORDERS AND GUILDS

The Order of Phosphorus is an initiatory guild dedicated to empowerment of the individual through willed activation of the Luciferian Path. Accomplishment on the Luciferian Path creates an opportunity for Prospective initiates to join the Black Order of the Dragon, a companion initiatory organization propagating Adversarial Magick and Vampyrism. There are numerous sub-orders within TOPH including "The Order of Set-Aapep", exploring Adversarial Egyptian and Luciferian Magick, "Ordo Azariel", a Vampyric-Qlippothic guild, "Ordo Algol", a Satanic-Chaos inspired magickal order and many others.

TOPH is also an initiatory order for women equally as well. At the close of 2008 TOPH announced the creation of THE DAUGHTERS OF LILITH, an initiatory system parallel to the traditional grades of TOPH however specifically focused on the Feminine Adversarial Current. This is perhaps one of the first initiatory orders focused on illuminating the Lilithian - Hekate current as well as the traditional Masculine.

The Order of Phosphorus is not a church: it is an Initiatic Order that includes diabolic atheists, theistic and pantheistic Satanists (and beyond). We do not regulate morality or metaphysics but instead focus on the acquiescence and wielding of power. How this differs from other organizations? This is your personal charge to investigate and research.

The Order has no restrictions on simultaneous membership with other organizations. Other organizations may prohibit your joining TOPH. Join where you will. The leadership and several initiates of the Ordo Luciferis [Luciferian Order of the Morning Star] dissolved/merged/joined into TOPH some years ago. It was less of an "official" action and more of a personal migration for the individuals now in TOPH.

There are no restrictions on being members of multiple groups on the TOPH level - only that materials received be kept in confidence / unpublished whether you remain a part of TOPH or not.

Any collaboration, joint study, research and magical brainstorming are highly encouraged within TOPH!!

BIBLIOGRAPHY

A.E. Waite……The Doctrine and Literature of the Kabalah

The Book of the Black Serpent

J.F.C. Fuller…..The Secret Wisdom of the Qabalah

S.L. MacGregor Mathers……..Kabbalah Unveiled

Westcott……Kabalah

Michael W. Ford……The Bible of the Adversary

Michael W. Ford……Liber HVHI

THE AUTHOR

Michael W. Ford is the head of several left hand path orders, centering on The Order of Phosphorus which serves as an initiatory guild for Luciferianism, from which Michael has written numerous books about. Mr. Ford is also head of The Black Order of the Dragon, a Vampyric Temple which is an inner order for TOPH, Order of Set-Aapep, a Typhonian and Sethian left hand path magickal guild, Ordo Azariel, a Vampyric Order based on the Qlippoth and the Church of Adversarial Light.

Mr. Ford is author of LUCIFERIAN WITCHCRAFT, LIBER HVHI – Magick of the Adversary, LUCIFERIAN GOETIA – Book of Howling, ADAMU – Luciferian Sex Magick, LUCIFERIAN TAROT with Nico Claux, BEGINNING LUCIFERIAN MAGICK, BOOK OF THE WITCH MOON – Chaos, Vampyric and Luciferian Sorcery, AKHKHARU- Vampyre Magick, SATANIC MAGICK – A Paradigm of Therion, GATES OF DOZAK – Primal Sorcery & the Book of the Worm, THE FIRST BOOK OF LUCIFERIAN TAROT, THE BIBLE OF THE ADVERSARY, MAGICK OF THE ANCIENT GODS – Chthonic Paganism and the Left Hand Path and more.

Mr. Ford is also an artist, having published an Art book entitled "RITES OF THE ANTICHRIST: The Art of Spiritual Lawlessness" which contains painting and images with blood, human bone dust, reptile and spider remains.

Michael W. Ford is also a musician having founded BLACK FUNERAL in the early 1990s, Psychonaut 75, Hexentanz and Valefor. Ford has also contributed to a soundtrack for a film called CADAVER BAY, HELLBOUND: Book of the Dead and currently records Ritual and Magickal music in a solo capacity.

Michael has an interest in Horror Fiction as well and is a co-owner of LUCIFERIAN APOTHECA, an online left hand path magickal shop.

DUALKARNAIN

Heirophage Dualkarnain is a current Priest in The Order of Phosphorus and is a dubious, shadowy character that excels at Qlippothic, Yatukih workings and has expanded as one who could devour Coronzon.

www.ingramcontent.com/pod-product-compliance
Lightning Source LLC
Chambersburg PA
CBHW021022090426
42738CB00007B/867